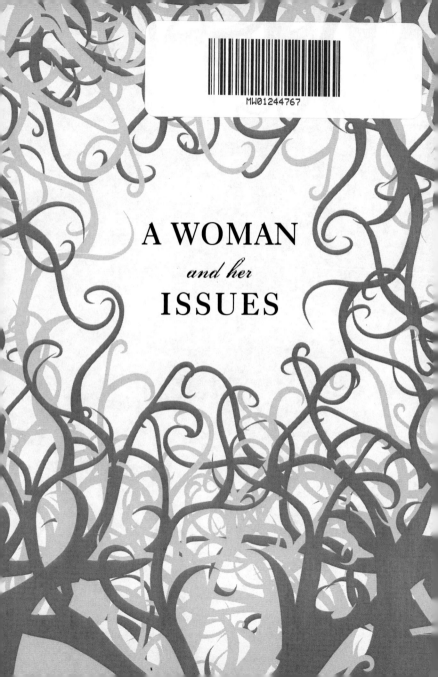

A WOMAN

and her

ISSUES

A WOMAN
and her
ISSUES

*getting to the root
of your problems*

by Rhonda B. Hurst

TATE PUBLISHING & *Enterprises*

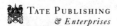

Tate Publishing is committed to excellence in the publishing industry. Our staff of highly trained professionals, including editors, graphic designers, and marketing personnel, work together to produce the very finest books available. The company reflects the philosophy established by the founders, based on Psalms 68:11,

"THE LORD GAVE THE WORD AND GREAT WAS THE COMPANY OF THOSE WHO PUBLISHED IT."

If you would like further information, please contact us:

1.888.361.9473 | www.tatepublishing.com

TATE PUBLISHING & *Enterprises*, LLC | 127 E. Trade Center Terrace

Mustang, Oklahoma 73064 USA

A Woman and Her Issues

Scripture quotations marked "KJV" are taken from the Holy Bible, King James Version, Cambridge, 1769. Used by permission. All rights reserved.

The opinions expressed by the author are not necessarily those of Tate Publishing, LLC.

This book is designed to provide accurate and authoritative information with regard to the subject matter covered. This information is given with the understanding that neither the author nor Tate Publishing, LLC is engaged in rendering legal, professional advice. Since the details of your situation are fact dependent, you should additionally seek the services of a competent professional.

Book design copyright © 2007 by Tate Publishing, LLC. All rights reserved.

Cover design by Leah LeFlore

Interior design by Lynly D. Taylor

Published in the United States of America

ISBN: 978-1-6024714-7-4

07.05.02

Dedicated to my late grandmother,
Rosie Jackson Farrow,
whose precious memories bring
me joy and sweet peace.
Each time that I look in the mirror,
I see her character, her morals, her spirit, her strength
and her wisdom; they all abide in me.
I pray that the presence of her memories
will continue to inspire me
to become the virtuous woman that
God has created me to be.
I pray that I will continue to overcome my
issues just as she conquered her issues.

ACKNOWLEDGMENTS

To my Lord and Savior, Jesus Christ who inspired me to write this book and share this message. Because of his unchanging love for me, I am able to testify that deliverance is still available for women and their issues.

To my family, friends and associates for their love, prayers, encouragement and support for this project.

To my son, Tyler Hurst whose unconditional love and adoration motivates me to dream, have ambitions, take risks and strive for excellence.

To Mrs. Delores Briggs for her editorial assistance in developing this manuscript.

Contents

INTRODUCTION

One day while sitting in my home reading God's Word, a passage of scriptures jumped into my spirit. God began to fill me with revelation knowledge regarding women and our many issues today. (Mark 5:25–34) I observed the woman with an issue of blood that had suffered for twelve years. There was no improvement to her condition. Instead, her issue grew worse. This woman spent all of her money seeing physicians that she thought could bring change to her situation. She was alienated from society, and we know that without society, it is impossible to have a normal social life. This leads me to believe that she was lonely, discouraged and at the end of her rope. She was sick and tired of being sick and tired. One day she heard Jesus was passing by and she pressed her way through the crowd and got close enough to touch Jesus' garments, and immediately her issue was no longer an issue. After twelve years of struggling, suffering and discomfort, her issue had been resolved. This biblical story still holds true for many women today. We have also been struggling and suffering with our issues for years. Instead of our issues getting better, it appears that they are growing worse. Whether they are physical, spiritual, mental, emotional or financial, our issues have been issues far too long.

Some women today are diligently seeking deliverance from their issues. Many of us receive counseling from the best psychiatrists. We give witness to Juanita Bynum's *No More Sheets,* Paula White's *Deal With It!,* Beth Moore's *Breaking Free,* and Joyce Meyer's *8 Ways to Keep the Devil Under Your Feet.* We attend T.D. Jakes' "Woman Thou Art Loosed" Conference every year. We also attend women symposiums and seminars for Self Empowerment, Building Self-Esteem, Health and Healing of Mind Body and Soul, Financial Recovery, and Tearing Down Strongholds. We confide in family and friends, allowing them to share their thoughts, beliefs and advice with us regarding our issues. Often, we pray and fast for ourselves. We constantly lay prostrate on the altar before the Lord. Yet, through it all, when it's over, said and done, we still permit the same issues, the same problems, the same people, and the same things to keep us stressed and depressed. God blesses us to wake up and see a brand new day; he sheds on us brand new mercies and gives us brand new opportunities. However, we are still combating with the same old issues day after day, week after week, month after month and year after year. We have been holding on to our issues for so long that now our issues are holding on to us.

This certain woman's story motivated and inspired me to write this book to help women address and conquer some of these issues that we deal with on a daily basis. Many women go through life feeling defeated, mistreated, used, abused, forsaken and forgotten because of their issues. I believe all women can relate and agree with this "certain woman;" we are also sick and tired of being sick and tired. We desire change, we want better than this; we simply want relief of our issues. Well, I've got good news for you and your issues! Jesus is still passing by! Deliverance is only one touch away. He's just waiting for us to press our way beyond our issues, problems and disbeliefs. He desires us to press beyond what we think and feel. Press beyond what people say to us and about us. We must press beyond our contentment and natural way of thinking. Jesus is standing by watching us look to our lovers, family members, TV evangelists, pastors, elders, priests, close friends and even psychiatrists to help us overcome our issues. He's hoping that we will soon realize that we have tried all the rest, and now it's time for us to try the best, which is Jesus Christ, our Lord and savior. God wants to do a new thing in women. He is simply raising the standards and elevating us to a higher level in Him. I'm a living witness that if you've got the faith, Jesus has the power to deliver, heal, save and loose us from the issues that hinder us from walking within the path God has ordained for our life.

My desire is that this book will touch the hearts of everyone reading it. My prayer is that it will help women better understand our "issues" and how to position our faith, our priorities, our mindsets and our God given authority to overcome these issues and live victoriously in Christ.

A CERTAIN WOMAN

And a certain woman, which had an issue of blood twelve years.

Mark 5:25

his "certain woman" is every woman I know. You may find it difficult to believe but all women have some kind of personal issue. Go ahead, lift up your hands and receive it in your spirit, you more than likely have a person, place or thing that you struggle with daily. I know how holy, sanctified and set apart you are, but girlfriend, you still have issues! Some women choose to pretend to be perfect. They act as if they have been righteous and holy all of their life. They want people to think that they live a perfect life, have a perfect marriage, possess the perfect job, raise perfect children, maintain perfect finances, surrounded by perfect friends, comes from a perfect past, and only think perfect thoughts. They give off this persona that because I'm a Christian, my life is issue free. Yeah right! On the other hand, you have women like me, which is not afraid to keep it real and willing to admit that although I'm an awesome woman of God, walking in anointing and operating in the authority of an evangelist, I still have issues that I'm in the process of being delivered from.

Many women have been deceived into thinking that once you commit your life to Christ, you immediately become issue free. You expect all of your problems and issues to disappear. Certainly not! Personally, I didn't realize I had so many issues until I got saved for real. When I got a dose of the real Holy Ghost and came from darkness into the marvelous light, God began to show me my ways. He put the spotlight on my thoughts, my words, my actions, my habits and my character. I had to acknowledge the fact that I was "a certain woman" with issues. I had some big issues and some little issues. I had some old issues that had been lingering for years and then I had some newly developing issues. I had spiritual issues, physical issues, marital issues, friendship issues, kinship issues, parental issues, career issues and financial issues. It was no secret to me that I needed some yesterday deliverance. I don't want you to ponder too much upon my issues right now. However, I want you to focus on the fact that I am a saved, sanctified and spirit-filled woman who knows without the shadow of a doubt that God is with me. He constantly manifests his power, majesty and dominion in my life. Nevertheless, I am still overcoming some issues. If you would just be true for a moment, you will find that your saved, sanctified, perfect self is still overcoming issues too.

Did you know that the biggest delay in our deliverance is denial? Notice how this woman claimed her issue. She acknowledged that she had a bleeding problem. In spite of what people thought and what society said about her, she claimed her issue. It is difficult for women to be delivered from issues when you continue to deny these issues exist within yourself. If your issue is stealing, say so. If your issue is a lying tongue, say so. If your issue is starting messes, say so. If your issue is whoremongering, drugs, loneliness, greed, obesity, low self-esteem or no self-esteem, selfishness, jealousy, fornication, adultery, depression, idolatry, over-spending, dead beat fathers, one bad relationship after another, shacking, a dirty mouth or whatever it is that separates you from God, just say so. It is crucial that we identify our issues and understand that they have the potential of becoming fatal distractions if we are not delivered and set free from them.

I find it disturbing that today's society and churches have misconstrued the "certain woman" with issues concept. We think women with issues are found outside the church walls. We view them as homeless women, walking the streets spaced out, living on the street corners begging for money or perhaps in crack houses, strung out and selling their bodies just to buy drugs. What? Many women come to church regularly with messed up minds, stony hearts and defiled temples. *(Romans 10:2) For I bear them record that they have a zeal of God, but not according to knowledge.* Over the years women have been taught how to act saved, how to look saved, how to dress saved, how to talk saved, how to walk saved, how to shout saved, how to sing saved and how to preach saved. We have been trained and educated to portray holiness without any real knowledge of God's Word and his way. As a result, many women are ashamed and embarrassed to admit that they have issues that they struggle with daily. They find it vital to cover up and ignore these issues for the sake of society and church politics. Some women think because you're suited and booted, dressed up in your beautiful white suit and big pretty hat, sitting in the front pew with your makeup painted on perfectly; you got your hair done, you're shouting, falling out and speaking in tongues, thinking that you have it going on. You attempt to convince everyone, including God that you don't have any issues. Let's go one step farther; some "certain women" have more dominant roles in the church. You are a woman of the clergy, the first lady, a missionary, a mother's board member, an usher, a choir director, a minister of music, a Sunday school teacher; this does not disqualify you from being that "certain woman" with issues.

As an evangelist, I see these certain women at every worship service, conference, workshop and symposium that I attend. I meet adulterers, liars, thieves, home wreckers, ditch diggers, trap setters, gossipers, backbiters, gamblers, haters, spectators, instigators, commentators and trouble-makers right in the church. I minister to promiscuous women. I chat with women that are recovering drug addicts. I talk with women that live with men and start a family yet the men refuse to marry them. I mingle with single mothers that are struggling to make ends meet without any support from the fathers. I come across women that perform sexual favors for money to ensure that the bills are paid. I converse with women that were robbed of their childhood due to incest, rape and molestation. I often console battered women that are being physically, sexually and emotionally abused by their husbands and lovers on a daily basis. I counsel with many women that have low self-esteem and some that have no self-esteem at all. I interact with women who are bashful and stand-offish because of physical imperfections. These are all certain women that I meet right in the church. If you look closely, you will find these certain women in your church and in every other church in America.

Society has also misrepresented women in the public eye. Not only do we veil women in the church from issues, we also veil the "certain women" in the public eye like Oprah Winfrey, Hillary Clinton, Laura Bush, Yolanda Adams, Celine Dion, Gabrielle Union, Mary J. Blige, Katie Couric and Tyra Banks, just to name a few. I have so much respect for these women. They are rich, famous, intelligent, talented and beautiful, but guess what? I'm convinced that they probably have issues. The media and tabloids constantly keep the spotlight on them and women like them in hopes of discovering their issues so that society can prejudge and condemn them for being that "certain woman" with issues. The truth is, whether you are a Christian woman, woman of the clergy, celebrity, super model, actress, anchor woman, recording artist or just an ordinary woman, you are human and you are the "certain woman" that I'm ministering to throughout this book. Beloved, regardless of your titles, accomplishments, social status, money and assets, how well you dress, what position you hold in the church, what car you drive, what size house you live in, this does not exempt you from having issues.

I want you to notice that the scriptures do not specify this certain woman's name, title, and employment background or salvation history. It merely refers to her as a "certain woman" with an issue. That's my point today. Your name, title, background, employer, church affiliation, bank account and social status are all irrelevant. Don't think for a moment that your titles, spirituality and social status will exempt you from issues. The truth is, even the best of us have hang-ups. This is nothing new to us. Eve was hard headed (Genesis 3). Sarah was impatient (Genesis 16). Hagar was kicked to the curb due to baby mama drama (Genesis 16). Rebekah was scheming (Genesis 27). Leah got played (Genesis 29). Rahab was a prostitute (Joshua 2). Jezebel was ruthless and controlling (I Kings). Delilah was devious (Judges 16). Hannah had to deal with baby mama drama. (I Samuel 2). Bathsheba was an adulterous woman (II

Samuel 11). Tamar was destitute after being raped by her own brother (II Samuel 13). Gomer was a straight up whore (Hosea 1). This is confirmation that women have been dealing with issues since the very beginning of creation, and to this day we still have issues that we need to be purged from to make certain that we become the woman that God has carefully created us to be; a woman of elegance, essence and excellence. It is important that we recognize our own individual struggles that we are constantly combating. It is time we take responsibility for the issues that we allow to keep us in bondage and distracted from our divine purpose.

Your Issue Is You

And a certain woman, which had an issue of blood twelve years, And had suffered many things of many physicians, and had spent all that she had, and was nothing bettered, but rather grew worse.

Mark 5:25–26

In the famous words of T.D. Jakes, "Get Ready, Get Ready, Get Ready" to be delivered from your "ISSUES." In the previous chapter, I ministered to your heart, but with this chapter I will minister directly to your issues. Often, when I'm done delivering a sermon, women (men too) will approach me and introduce themselves or commend the sermon. I might ask them questions like "Are you saved?", "Do you know Jesus?", "Do you want to be delivered?", "What do you want from the Lord today?" and people will begin telling me their life's story. They go all the way back to sixth grade, when Aunt Hattie Mae buried

Uncle Slim. They start telling me about their evictions, foreclosures, divorces, abusive relationships, backbiting friends, addictions, learning disabilities, etc. The stories go on and on and on. I have to keep coaxing them back to the question to address the real issue. This is a polished way of not addressing the issue at hand. Let's look at the woman caught in the very act of adultery.

> ¹*Jesus went unto the mount of Olives.* ²*And early in the morning he came again into the temple, and all the people came unto him; and he sat down, and taught them.* ³*And the scribes and Pharisees brought unto him a woman taken in adultery; and when they had set her in the midst,* ⁴*They say unto him, Master, this woman was taken in adultery, in the very act.* ⁵*Now Moses in the law commanded us, that such should be stoned: but what sayest thou?* ⁶*This they said, tempting him, that they might have to accuse him. But Jesus stooped down, and with his finger wrote on the ground, as though he heard them not.* ⁷*So when they continued asking him, he lifted up himself, and said unto them, He that is without sin among you, let him first cast a stone at her.* ⁸*And again he stooped down, and wrote*

on the ground. ⁹And they which heard it, being convicted by their own conscience, went out one by one, beginning at the eldest, even unto the last: and Jesus was left alone, and the woman standing in the midst. ¹⁰When Jesus had lifted up himself, and saw none but the woman, he said unto her, Woman, where are those thine accusers? hath no man condemned thee? ¹¹She said, No man, Lord. And Jesus said unto her, Neither do I condemn thee: go, and sin no more.

John 8:1–11

Notice how Jesus dealt with the issue only. He didn't investigate to see if the woman was married or if she was single and the man was married. He never asked how long the affair had been going on or why she was involved in an adulterous relationship. Also notice that Jesus did not discuss her issue with the instigators and accusers that apprehended her. He basically identified that she had committed sin and had gotten caught. He dealt with the issue that all of the by-standers had also committed sin and they were not worthy to throw stones. Jesus forgave her and told her to go and sin no more. He only dealt with the issue at hand! Women, we need to handle our issues like Jesus. Stop dwelling on the preliminaries of your issues: who, what, when, where, how and why. Quit making excuses and justifying your issues. You are denying your real issue which in turn delays your deliverance.

Now, I'm getting ready to bless you real good! In the famous words of Bishop Eddie Long, "Watch this, Watch this, Watch this!" Biblically, the certain woman's issue was the flowing or discharge of blood. With women today, our issues are unsettled matters that we have chosen not to settle.

Do this exercise with me... say the word issue slowly to yourself and then say it out loud. Listen carefully to the content of the word "issue." Say it "is you," "is you." Do you see where I'm going with this? It's You. The root cause of most of your problems is you! Go ahead and receive it... "IT'S YOU."

When I first started counseling people, I had lots of patience. I could sit and listen to women go on and on about their many issues. However, the more I began to read and understand God's Word, it was impossible for me to listen to the whining, complaining, finger pointing and venting without giving them words of truth... "It's You!" Women hate those words, but we must know the truth and the truth will set us free. *(John 8:32)* No more excuses! No more denial! No more sugar coating!

No more justifying! No more games! Your real issue "IS YOU." It's you that focuses so much on your problems that you fail to find solutions. We have a peculiar way of looking at our unsettled matters. I relate back to the certain woman's issue of blood. In her mind, the issue was the flowing out or discharge of blood. However, when we look closely at her testimony, the real issue was she had not exercised faith in Jesus. She had exercised faith in the physicians and many different concoctions, but her issue was still an issue steadily growing worse. Once she exercised faith in Jesus, it was then that the bleeding stopped. It was then that she was healed and made whole. Allow me to expound upon some of our "It's Yous" that women deal with today.

"IT'S YOU" ISSUES

SINGLENESS ISSUES... Your issue is not loneliness or being unmarried! It's you that put your life on hold because you don't have a spouse. It's you that's too embarrassed to go to the theater alone. It's you that has to have someone special in your life to feel complete. It's you that's willing to settle for anybody for the sake of having a man. It's you that can't wait for God to send you Mr. Right. Therefore, you settle for Mr. Right Now. Mr. Right Now is exactly that, here right now with no plans of sticking around for the future.

> *⁶Be careful for nothing; but in every thing by prayer and supplication with thanksgiving let your requests be made known unto God. ⁷And the peace of God, which passeth all understanding, shall keep your hearts and minds through Christ Jesus. ⁸Finally, brethren, whatsoever things are true, whatsoever things are honest, whatsoever things are just, whatsoever things are pure, whatsoever things are lovely, whatsoever things are of good report; if there be any virtue, and if there be any praise, think on these things.*

Philippians 4:6–8

Chill out! Make your requests known to God that you desire companionship. Then relax and enjoy your life to the fullest. Treat yourself to dinner and a movie! Go on a cruise! Take a trip to Paris! If you can't afford Paris, Cancun or the Bahamas would be nice too. Go someplace you've always wanted to visit. Do something out of the ordinary that you've always wanted to do. Discover a new hobby. Establish a new hangout spot that is diversified. Stella got her groove back, now you go and get yours.

In due season, God will bless you with Mr. Right. The key words here are "due season." Some single women are waiting for a husband. However, you have not prepared yourself for marriage. Therefore, you have not arrived into your due season. I hear women stressing the fact that they are ready to settle down but they don't know how to cook. Some of them still live at home with Mama and Daddy. They do not have stable employment. Some don't have their own transportation. Their credit is horrendous. The truth is many single women have not positioned and prepared themselves for marriage. Back in the day, men were looking for wives to love them, take care of the house and raise the children while they worked and provided for the family. Men today are looking for women that also have something to bring to the table. I'm not saying that men don't want to take care of their wives, but men are looking for women that have something to offer as a wife. Let me share a secret with single women... the reason so many of us are single is because we expect men to have all the following: financial security, a good job, a nice house and a fancy car. We want men to be goal oriented, well dressed with good morals and respectable. Well this is what men want from women also. Beloved, successful men are seeking successful women. Successful men are seeking helpmates not free loaders. Men want women that will build them up not tear them down. Successful men desire women that will help them progress not digress. Before you arrive in your "due season" there is work to be done. Acquire a job that offers stable income and benefits. Purchase your own home or get your own place, clear up unnecessary debt such as medical bills, student loans and credit cards, etc. Learn the basic domestic skills that are required to maintain a husband, marriage and household like budgeting, cooking, cleaning, and washing. Just as you want the man you marry to be responsible and established, you should also be responsible and established. Trust me, when you prove to God that you are worthy of a husband and you can handle the responsibilities of marriage, he will bless you with the man that he has perfectly created and carefully chosen just for you. It will be the man that God has equipped to minister to you physically, spiritually, emotionally and financially.

Many singles are not struggling with singleness. Their real issue is celibacy. In talking with single women (men too), I hear the same question: "How do I live saved, single and celibate?" We have mastered the

part of living saved and single. However, we struggle
with being celibate while waiting on God. The truth
is, in divine context, if you are saved, single and living
a life for the Lord you should be celibate. All three go
hand in hand. However, celibacy is a struggle for most
saved and single women. When I was married I would
tell single people to "Hold On," "Wait On God," "Be
Patient," "Keep Yourself." Now that I'm in the singles'
boat, I see that it is not that simple especially when you
date saved and single people that aren't committed to
celibacy. In order for women to live saved, single and
celibate, we must change our view on sex. We can't continue to think that sex is just a physical act. Sex is spiritual. Maybe sex is physical for someone who does not
acknowledge God as their personal Savior. However,
sex for the born again believer is spiritual.

> [15]*Know ye not that your bodies are the members of
> Christ? shall I then take the members of Christ,
> and make them the members of an harlot? God
> forbid.* [16]*What? know ye not that he which is
> joined to an harlot is one body? for two, saith
> he, shall be one flesh.* [17]*But he that is joined unto
> the Lord is one spirit.* [18]*Flee fornication. Every
> sin that a man doeth is without the body; but he*

that committeth fornication sinneth against his own body. [19]What? know ye not that your body is the temple of the Holy Ghost which is in you, which ye have of God, and ye are not your own? [20]For ye are bought with a price: therefore glorify God in your body, and in your spirit, which are God's.

1 Corinthians 6:15–20

If we confess to be saved and single, God demands purity. I know being celibate can be difficult, but as a saved, born again believer in Christ you have the authority to put your cravings for sex under submission until God blesses you to marry! (1 John 4:4) *Greater is he that is in me than he that is in the world.* Our lives as Christians are a living witness to others, and we cannot break the laws of God without hindering others from coming to Christ. We must live our lives in purity before a sinful and wicked world. We should not be living according to society's standards but according to God's standard in the Bible.

I want to encourage single women to see the blessing in singleness. It is an important time to prepare us for marriage. It can also be a time to experience a closer communion with God. Eventually, in God's plan and timing, He will bless us with a wonderful mate so that both lives can be a witness for Him. There are worse things than being alone. One of these is to be out of God's will by compromising and marrying someone who does not feel the same way we do about the Lord.

DATING ISSUES...Dating is not your real issue! It's you that doesn't understand the dating game. Why is dating so difficult for women? Here's what I've found. Dating is designed for two people to get to know each other on a more social and personal basis to identify if there is a possibility for a relationship. However, women in today's society want to skip the getting to know each other and cut right to the chase of sex and marriage. Yep, that's right, after two or three dates you want to put exclusive rights on the man. Certainly not! You don't know if you are really compatible or not. You don't know if you have some of the same interests. You get busy selecting your bridal party and your wedding scheme and you've only had your third date and when the man you are dating stops calling you and starts ignoring your calls then you are devastated and heart-broken. This is absurd! Unless a man tells you that he wants to indulge in a committed relationship with you, you are just dating! No strings attached! Contrary to what women may believe, there's a huge difference between dating and being in a committed relationship. Trust me, just because a man takes you to dinner doesn't mean you are the only woman he wants to eat out with. Have you noticed how men don't get bent out of shape because you don't call them after a date? Most women freak out when they go on a date and the man doesn't call them on a regular basis after the date. Many women are heartbroken! For crying out loud, it was only a date! Personally, I feel women should date like a man. Go on your date knowing that it is only a date. You should have fun and enjoy your date's company and call it a night. No strings attached! If he calls to schedule another date with you... fine. If not, don't you dare call him to see why he didn't call you. Perhaps he wasn't that into you! Oh well. NEXT! Stop sitting by that phone waiting for him to call; it was only a date! I'm not encouraging women to go on a dating binge. However, I am encouraging women to have options and to keep an open mind about dating. Beloved, I know it is easy to get attached to men that you enjoy spending time with. I also know how difficult it can be finding a man that you really enjoy dating. However, we can't be so overbearing and demanding of his time that we scare him off. Regardless, if he's a great catch, he must want you to be the woman that catches him.

Let's talk about another issue with dating. It's you that thinks inside the box. Personally, I feel single women in today's society have so many dating issues because of their personal mental margins. Some women refuse to date men in the workplace. Some women only date men in their church. Some women only date men that are tall, slender and handsome. Some women only date men that are short, thick and average looking. Some women only date men of their own race. Some women only date younger men. Some women only date older men. Some women only date athletic men. Some women only date rich men. Women, wake up and step outside of the box. Cross the line a little bit. Have you ever thought that your dream man just might not come packaged the way you want him? You might find true love in someone younger than you. Your most enjoyable date could very well be with someone of a different race. Your soul mate just might be opposite of what you imagine, but you'll never know if you only date within "your" margins. I am so tired of women saying, "It's hard to find good men worth dating." I beg to differ. It's you that places restrictions on your definition of "a good man." Beloved, open your mind. So what he's a little shorter. So what he's a little younger. Perhaps he's a little older. So what he's not as cute as you would like him to be. So what he's outside of your origin. Remember, it's just a date. See what happens!

RELATIONSHIP ISSUES... Your issue is not one bad relationship after another, it's you that doesn't understand the people that you are trying to relate with. Isn't it funny how the most important lessons in life are not taught in school? We learn so many different things while in school. However, how to successfully build and maintain perfect relationships was not one of them. Nobody teaches us, for example, about relationships: how to choose a partner, how to stay together despite differences, and how to love unconditionally. For most women, it seems, learning about relationships is a matter of trial-and-error, often with a lot of pain and heartache mixed in. I speak with women who have had relationships with different men but they all have the same disastrous outcome. One moment things are going great and the next moment the relationship takes a nose dive. I find it disturbing that so many women are suffering from bad relationships.

I'll be the first to admit that I too struggle with relationship issues. However, I have confirmed what the real issue is within me. You see it is simple. I'm a very intimate person and I've tried to manage and maintain relationships with men that do not fully understand what intimacy is. You can't embrace what you don't understand. Let's look closely at the word (intimacy). This is what I gather (in to me see). Yes, this is what I need: intimacy. I need my mate to see into me as I see into him. Once we begin to see into each others' lives, hearts, dreams, ambitions, needs and desires, then we will be able to successfully relate to one another in the relationship. Some men find me too deep. Okay! Maybe I am. However, it doesn't mean I'm not a good catch. It simply means I need to possess a relationship with a deep mate or someone that can relate to my deepness. Laughing!

My girlfriends accuse me of wanting the "fairy tale" relationship. Okay! Guilty as charged! Forgive me for wanting my mate to see so clearly into my heart that he knows how to secure his place in it. Forgive me for wanting a mate that can see so clearly into my heart that he sees how fragile it is and disciplines himself not to break it. Forgive me for wanting a mate to see so clearly into my mind that he intercepts my worries, concerns and insecurities. Forgive me for yearning for a mate that can see so clearly in my spirit that my presence walks with him when we are apart. Forgive me for needing a mate that can see so clearly into my spirit that he intercedes in prayer for my strength as I do the works of God, who has sent me. Forgive me for craving a mate that can see so clearly into my physical needs that he satisfies me in every aspect, leaving no room for third party distractions. Forgive me for wanting my mate to see so clearly into my dreams that he assists in making them come true. Forgive me for wanting a mate that is equipped to minister to a minister. Forgive me for desiring a man that sees so clearly into me that his presence compliments my character. I've decided not to waste my time with men that are not willing to be intimate in a relationship with me. It is impossible to have a healthy, happy and successful relationship with someone that can't see into you. If you can't see into me, there's no way you can make a commitment to me. Beloved, define what you are seeking in a relationship. Identify what you are willing to bring to a relationship. Set guidelines and standards for your relationship. If your mate can't deal with that, let him walk. If the relationship doesn't fit, don't force it.

Not only do women struggle in relationships with

their mates, they also find themselves struggling to maintain harmony within their family and friends circle. It's troubling when I talk to women that are not on speaking terms with their parents, siblings and close friends. We must ask ourselves one question: Why is it so hard to relate to those we love? Allow me to help set you free.

Communication—Women have mastered the "silent treatment." When we have disagreements with our mates, family members and friends, we believe the solution is just to be silent. As a result, sometimes we live years without speaking to those we love. Contrary to what you believe, silence is not the answer. I feel the longer people go without speaking, the harder it becomes to mend the relationship. You must find a technique of cooling off and then calmly express your feelings and try not to judge the other people involved when they express their feelings to you.

Approach with empathy—Stop being so hard! Put yourself in the other person's shoes. Understand that he or she has emotional wounds and is hurting as well.

Seek compromise—The goal is to resolve your differences by reaching an understanding that allows both people to come out ahead. You can't always have it your way. Grow up! You must understand that not everyone may share your same beliefs. What works best for you may not work best for your mate, parents, siblings and friends. What seems logical to you may not be logical to someone else.

Offer Forgiveness—This does *not* mean excusing abusive behavior or staying with an abuser. Forgiving means letting go of a need to hurt back. Anger only accumulates and harms us, emotionally and physically. Forgiveness is a gift to yourself as well as to your broken relationship. Sometimes we are reluctant to forgive because we are simply tired of the relationship. Remember, that you may forgive people in your past (without taking them back or letting them play an active role in your life).

Beloved, relationships, like all good things, require effort. Due to our many different personalities and life experiences, we are subject to clash with those we love from time to time. Be patient and allow for mistakes and misunderstandings. Know that a change in one person can have an impact on every aspect of the relationship. Lastly, don't be afraid to seek professional counseling if you need it.

DIVORCE ISSUES... Your issue is not a broken marriage or being a divorcee. It's you that can't get over your feelings of rejection. It's you that ignores the words "Final Divorce Decree!" It's you that tries to hold on to a marriage that no longer exists. It's you harboring bitterness. It's you losing weight and crying yourself to sleep every night. It's you that wonders what woulda, coulda and shoulda happened differently. Let's think about this realistically. Marriage is the joining together of husband and wife. Joining together also means connecting one to another. Divorce is the legal disconnection of the marriage. Too many divorced women are still spiritually, physically and mentally connected to a legally disconnected union. For instance, if my telephone is disconnected and I try to use it, my efforts will be in vain because there is no connection. So it is with you and the "ex;" there's no connection. As a result of this disconnection, your time, efforts and attention are all in vain. A man that is disconnected from you will constantly disrespect you, ignore you, hurt you and walk over you. Your needs and desires are irrelevant to him. When this disconnection occurs, the spouse is no longer good for you! Girlfriend, hang it up! The thrill is gone! The marriage has been disconnected. It is finished! Now it's time for you to snap out of it and get delivered. Trust me, I know it is easier said than done because I've been there, done that and got a tee-shirt for it! Okay! I consider myself to be a certified divorcee because I survived a divorce after fourteen years of marriage. I discovered the keys to overcoming divorce, and I would like to share those three keys with you. Grieve, Forgive and Let It Go!

- Grieve…It's okay to cry. Let it out! Your tears are part of the healing process. I cried many nights, but after the tears stopped rolling, I found myself better, stronger and ready to move to the next level of my life.

- Forgive…You will be judged by how you treat people not how people treat you. You don't have to be friends with the "ex," but you don't have to be enemies either. Just as God forgives us, we must learn to forgive others. I can imagine that hurt and pain that one suffers when betrayed by the one they love. However, forgiveness is the first step to deliverance.

- Let It Go…Get over it! Release it! Move On!

This is exactly what I did. Every time I thought about the "ex" or began to throw myself a pity party, I would recite the words "Grieve, Forgive and Let It Go." It took a while, but pretty soon I had grieved, forgave and let him go. It wasn't easy getting past my divorce issues. I was literally a walking emotional rollercoaster! I had some days when I was crying and sad. Some days I was shouting and glad. Some days I was mad and bitter. Some days I was in denial and shock. Some days I was just happy to be free from a man that had repeatedly hurt me throughout our marriage. There were days that I wanted to sleep all day to keep from worrying about bills. There were some days that I would spend hours standing in front of the mirror trying to figure out whether or not I was still desirable (I am!). Some days I isolated myself from family and friends. I was afraid to attend church services because I didn't know how my church family would react. My biggest fear was that I wouldn't be accepted as an evangelist (I am). I had to tell myself, "It's You." I thank God, I was delivered and set free from my divorce issues. I now stand in agreement with Apostle Paul.

> [13]*Brethren, I count not myself to have apprehended: but this one thing I do, forgetting*

*those things which are behind, and reaching
forth unto those things which are before, [14]I press
toward the mark for the prize of the high calling
of God in Christ Jesus.*

Philippians 3:13–14

Of course, I don't expect you to forget about the "ex" because of the many fond memories that you hold in your heart. However, you can't be consumed and diverted by a marriage that no longer exists. Beloved, you need to stay focused on where you are right now in your life, so you will know where God is trying to take you in the future. I feel that every divorced woman in America should see Tyler Perry's movie Diary of a Mad Black Woman. It proves the old saying that "one man's junk is another man's treasure." You should always remember that divorce disconnects you from the marriage, not from life, society and your new beginning.

MARRIED WITH CHILDREN ISSUES... Not having private time for yourself is not your real issue. It's you trying to function as if you are a robot. It's you thinking you have to walk in the shoes of Superwoman. It's you that refuses to delegate household chores to your husband and children. It's you that doesn't make time to pamper yourself. It's you that feels you're not a good mother unless you attend every boy and girl's scout meeting. You feel obligated to attend every piano and dance recital, every little league baseball and basketball game that your child participates in. It's you that beats yourself up if you are unable to accompany your children on school field trips. Not only can your children require and demand a significant amount of your time, so can your hubby. Sometimes they can be big babies, too. Your social circle can be overwhelming also with birthday parties, anniversary celebrations, baby showers, dinner parties, workplace events and church activities; what law says you have to attend all of them? Girlfriend, it's you that won't balance your time appropriately. Learn to just say No! I know that responsibilities come with being married and raising children. I know you have a career and a social life. However, I feel that every married woman, especially those with children and careers should take a day each week to relax, relate and release. Women should pick one day a week to sleep late, laugh loud and dance like no one is watching! At least twice a month, you should pamper yourself with a trip to the beauty salon. Get a manicure and a pedicure. Perhaps you should go to dinner with just your husband or lunch with your girlfriends. You should even consider a few hours at the spa; get yourself a therapeutic or a Swedish massage. Maybe you should just steal away and read a good book. This will keep you rejuvenated, restored, and sane. Women that are married with children often have to wear quite a few hats. You are known as wife, mama, banker, cook, laundry lady, maid, chauffer, counselor, handy man, nurse, teacher, hairstylist and minister. Sometimes we get so wrapped up in being everything to everybody that we lose ourselves. Beloved, don't lose yourself. If necessary, keep a personal calendar to help you balance time for God, your spouse, your children and yourself.

ADULTERY ISSUES...Cheating is not your issue! It's you that likes the thrill of cheating. It's you that gets a kick out of wrecking homes. It's you that's content being the other woman. It's you that enjoys the secret lovers' setup. (Matthew 5:27) Ye have heard that it was said by them of old time, Thou shalt not commit adultery. Now I'm saying it: Thou shall not commit adultery! Whether you are married and cheating or if you are single and cheating with a man that is married. Cheating ultimately leads to destruction. Marriages, lives, dreams, hopes and futures can all be destroyed

by insignificant affairs. Women, I understand that
there are some fine, good looking, intelligent, rich,
well groomed married men walking around on earth.
However, we must look at the big picture, they belong
to someone else. Therefore, back off, stay in your place,
focus on your own husband and leave other women's
property alone!

I had the opportunity to minister to a woman that
had been involved with a married man for years. She
finally convinced him to leave his wife and children to
pursue a life with her. She had played an intricate part
in the demolishing of his previous marriage and years
later, they seemed to have the picture perfect marriage,
children, home and careers. However, one day, she
was forced to recollect the day this man left his wife
and children and started a life with her. She felt hurt,
embarrassed remorseful and ashamed. She wept un-
controllably! Reason being, eight years into their marriage, he left her and their children to start a life with
someone new. She informed me that she never saw it
coming. She thought they were happily married and
would be happy until death parted them. (Galatians
6:7) *Be not deceived; God is not mocked: for whatsoever a
man soweth, that shall he also reap.* It is detrimental for
women to go through life not considering the conse-

quences and repercussions of adulterous relationships. Things may work out for a moment. You may enjoy marital bliss for years, but girlfriend, if you sow it, you will reap it! Okay! If a man cheats with you, more than likely he'll cheat on you!

On the other hand some married women are the ones doing the cheating. I had the opportunity of meeting an interesting young man. He's an entrepreneur, very attractive, saved and filled with the Holy Spirit. He has a smile that will light up any dark room. This man's goal in life was to please God so that he would know how to please his wife and family. He supported his wife's dreams unconditionally. He never forgot her birthday or their anniversary. He would send her flowers just because. Every time he would hear about a new perfume, he would purchase it for her to try out. If she didn't have time to do the house cleaning, he would hire a maid service to come in and clean so his wife wouldn't have to. He would treat her to the beauty salon and nail shop every Saturday morning. Did I mention the random shopping sprees he afforded her? Words cannot describe his credentials as a father. Nevertheless, after eleven years of marriage his wife decided she wanted someone else. Although he was giving her the world, she fell in love with someone else. She began to pursue a relationship with a man that she felt was better for her. He had all the right moves and said all the right things. She was so enamored over this new man that she asked for a divorce. She wanted to move on with her life and marry the man of her dreams. After her decision to leave her husband and move in with her new honey, she discovered that she gave up a good husband for a "NO" man. She discovered that her dream man had no job, no income, no house, no car, no dreams and no goals which left them with no future. Can you say "Certified Loser?" She lost so much to gain so little.

I find it amazing that women are still falling for the oldest trick in the book. Satan paints this pretty picture that the grass is greener on the other side. He cons you into thinking your man on the side is so much better than the husband you have at home. Women will begin to play the comparison game; he touches me better, he listens to me better, he understands me better, he makes love better. Duh… that's how the picture is painted. Trust me when I tell you that the grass is never greener on the other side. It is our desire to graze in the grass that makes it so green. Beloved, marriage is so beautiful. (Hebrews 13:4) *Marriage is honorable in all, and the bed undefiled: but whoremongers and adulterers*

God will judge. Married women get in your place. Stay focused on your husband and the vows that you made to him before God. (I Corinthians 7:3) *Let the husband render unto the wife due benevolence: and likewise also the wife unto the husband.* I would never tell a woman to stay in a marriage in which she is not being treated fairly or getting the respect that she deserves. However, I beseech women to love, honor and cherish their husbands that successfully walk in their role of head of the house, father, provider and protector. We must stop falling for Satan's same old trick of seduction!

Today Satan is still playing the seduction game to deceive us into exploring adulterous relationships. He's been doing it since the beginning of creation, and we have been falling for it since the beginning of creation.

> [1]*Now the serpent was more subtil than any beast of the field which the LORD God had made. And he said unto the woman, Yea, hath God said, Ye shall not eat of every tree of the garden?* [2]*And the woman said unto the serpent, We may eat of the fruit of the trees of the garden:* [3]*But of the fruit of the tree which is in the midst of the garden, God hath said, Ye shall not eat of it, neither shall*

ye touch it, lest ye die. ⁴And the serpent said unto the woman, Ye shall not surely die: ⁵For God doth know that in the day ye eat thereof, then your eyes shall be opened, and ye shall be as gods, knowing good and evil. ⁶And when the woman saw that the tree was good for food, and that it was pleasant to the eyes, and a tree to be desired to make one wise, she took of the fruit thereof, and did eat, and gave also unto her husband with her; and he did eat.

Genesis 3:1–6

Can you say tricked, hoodwinked and bamboozled? The devil is the master of lies and deceit. I find it fascinating that women still fall for married men's lies of seduction:

- *"I really love you"*… Certainly not! Married men that cheat are greedy and selfish. They will confess love for any woman that feeds into their demonic spirit of adultery. I feel that a man that really loves a woman will keep her in the will of God instead of enticing her to go contrary to it.

- *"My body is with my wife but my heart is with you"*… Certainly not! *(Matthew 6:21) For where your treasure is, there will your heart be also.* If you are involved with a married man and you have his "heart" but his wife has all of his treasures, you are in for a rude awakening. Be not deceived, for if his treasures are with his wife, his heart is there too. Any man can give you his heart but very few will give you access to his treasures.

• *"I'm not happy"*… Certainly not! Women are strong willed and are built to endure. Women will stay in an unhappy marriage for years for the sake of their children, financial stability and fear of change. However, men are somewhat different. An unhappy man will leave you quicker than a cat will jump a ditch. He'll leave with no second thoughts. Knowing this, if a married man is still living at home with his wife and family, he is happy. He may not be as happy some days as others but overall, he's happy. He just wants to have his cake and a little ice cream on the side. All women know what happens with ice cream, it doesn't take long for it to melt.

Adulterous women, use your brain and quit acting

insane. You are mature enough to see straight through these tired old tricks of seduction. Single women, you deserve to have a man of your own, not someone else's man that you can only borrow from time to time.

I do feel that I should address the women that are victims of adulterous affairs. Being a victim of adultery myself, I can speak boldly when I say adultery is an awful thing to go through. It hurts! You develop issues of distrust, insecurity, paranoia and humiliation. You try to analyze what you did wrong. The truth is you didn't do anything wrong. Your spouse attempted to find something that he mistakenly thought he was missing in his marriage. As a result, you find yourself feeling the hurt and pain of an insignificant affair. Beloved, you are not alone. Trust me, you are not the first woman and you certainly will not be the last woman on earth to experience infidelity. Life goes on! If you find it in your heart to forgive your husband and make the marriage work, put the pain behind you and move forward with your lives together! Have you ever noticed a cut or scrape on your skin? At first it bleeds, it hurts and it is sore when you touch it. However, after a while it begins to heal. If you don't pick at it, the wounded area is eventually restored. Often victims of adultery say that they forgive their spouse but yet they continue to pick at the wounded area. You want to ask questions, analyze the affair, and discuss the details. A word of advice: stop it! This only opens up old wounds. Grieve, Forgive and Let It Go! You can't move forward in your marriage as long as you dwell in the past.

PROMISCUITY ISSUES... The love of sex is not your issue. It's you trying to fill a void that's missing in your life. It's you that thinks you have to compromise your body to get a man's attention. It's you that thinks sex is the only way to man's heart. It's you that thinks your sex is so good you need to share it with every man you date. It's you that allows worthless men to defile your precious temple. (I Corinthians 3:16–17) 16*Know ye not that ye are the temple of God, and that the Spirit of God dwelleth in you? 17If any man defile the temple of God, him shall God destroy; for the temple of God is holy, which temple ye are.*

Personally, I feel the reason so many women struggle with promiscuity issues is because they can't distinguish the difference between dating and being in a committed relationship. It is the nature of women to latch on to men that they enjoy spending time with. However, the truth is that some men just want to take you out and spend time with you. They are not trying to go to the chapel. Therefore, women should stop feeling compelled to sleep with men because they buy you dinner. Dinner is just dinner! A movie is just a movie! A gift is just a gift! Remember, it's only a date! All of these things are nice but they are not sex vouchers. These are simple notions to let a woman know that he's interested in spending time with you. Often we give up too much, too soon, and before we know it, we are back in the sheets. Women should raise the standards and follow the rule of No Contract, No Contact. Promiscuous behavior communicates to the male mind that you are easy, cheap and docile. My late grandmother, Rosie Farrow, would always share her wisdom with me when I was a teenager. She told me something that I never forgot. She said, "Things that come easy aren't worth having." This is so true! Men will make a promiscuous woman his trick but most of the time he will not make her his wife. Beloved, save yourself for the man that earns your love not just any man that feels he deserves it. All men think they deserve your sexual attention. It's their stinking thinking nature. Rest assured that if you respect yourself and your body, men will have to respect you and your body.

I hear promiscuous women using the term "casual

sex." I think we should change the term to "casualty sex" because women are dying everyday from HIV/AIDS. There is nothing casual about that. HIV/AIDS has become an epidemic in America. Society elects to believe that this is an epidemic in Africa. Certainly not! HIV/AIDS is out of control in America. STDs (Sexually Transmitted Diseases) are so widespread that the statistics are shocking. I once read an article in the *San Francisco Chronicle* that stated there are twelve million new cases of STDs annually in the United States. 100,000 to 150,000 women become infertile each year as a result of STDs. Other women endure years of pain as some of these diseases are incurable. What a tragic price to pay for promiscuity. Perhaps your promiscuous way of thinking is telling you that you will never be a statistic. Beloved, if you play with fire long enough, you will eventually get burned.

INDEPENDENT ISSUES... Being self-sufficient is not your issue. It's you that won't step back and let a man do some things that they pleasure in doing for you. Being independent is a good thing. I'm sure Ms. Independent knows how to change a flat tire and change the oil in her vehicle. Yes, you pay your own bills. Yes, you can treat yourself to dinner and a movie. Yes, you can buy nice gifts for yourself. This is great! However, don't be so independent that you can't appreciate the assistance of a good man. When talking with independent women, they all say the same thing; men that are nice and helpful are looking for something in return. Or, they are trying to be helpful to, in turn, gain control and rule over women. It's sad to say that many of them are. However, some men are just genuinely concerned about you and want to be there for you to help make life a little bit easier. They take pleasure in picking up the tab, opening doors for you, washing your vehicle, painting your house, cutting your grass, changing a light bulb. Being too independent is an issue for me. I'll be the first to confess that I'm Ms. Independent in the worst way but I'm working on it. After my divorce, I didn't want to give any man the satisfaction of thinking I needed him to do anything for me. I was determined to prove the point that I can make it on my own, all by myself. It didn't take me long to get over that. Beloved, it's okay to be aware of men trying to get over on you. However, it is also okay for you to let your guard down for ones who are not.

GHETTO ISSUES...Living in the ghetto is not your issue. It's you that allows the ghetto to live in you. I know many women that have never lived in the ghetto. As a matter of fact, they reside in beautiful homes, prestigious neighborhoods and drive nice cars. Many of them are highly educated with degrees, but they have ghetto-like tendencies. On the other hand, I've met women who grew up in housing projects. They did not enjoy the finer things in life as children. However, just observing them you would never know it because they are so polished, well-spoken, elegant and disciplined. Personally, I view ghetto women as being loud, unruly, rough around the edges and lacking finesse. Often, ghetto women find it necessary to overdo it with makeup, jewelry, tattoos, body piercing, hairstyles and revealing clothing. Some ghetto women have established their own lingo. In general conversation, their Ebonics, slang and incorrect grammar will make your head spin. Don't get me wrong, I'm not downing or judging women with ghetto-like tendencies. I'm simply trying to keep it real and deal with a real issue in today's society; our country is in desperate need of queens. Contrary to what a "ghetto" woman believes, a real man wants a lady. Yes, a man may want a ghetto woman in the bedroom. Yes, he might want to kick it around his house with a ghetto fabulous woman. However, when it's time to take it to the streets, a real man wants a lady on his arm. I'm not signifying that ghetto women don't deserve to be taken out to a fancy restaurant, corporate functions, jazz clubs, Sunday morning worship or home to meet mama. What I am saying is that men are very selective when it comes to their public image. Beloved, if you are reading this book and you know you have ghettoriffic characteristics, please do me a favor and tone it down and act like the queen that God created you be. Cover up your body! You can wear sexy clothing without revealing all of your assets. Leave something for a man's imagination. Lose the wild hairstyles too, and take it easy on the makeup! Hairstyles and makeup are designed to enhance your beauty not destroy it. Let the English language be your primary language when in public. Leave Ebonics, profanity, slang and other bad grammar at home behind closed doors. Better yet, leave them alone!

SELF-ESTEEM ISSUES...Low self-esteem is not your real issue. It's you that allows magazines and television commercials to define true beauty. It's you that's intimidated by your physical imperfections. It's you that constantly remind yourself of childhood hurts and disappointments. It's you that doesn't understand that beauty is found within. It's you that has very little value of your life and your purpose in the earth.

Building self-esteem is the first step towards your happiness and a better life. Self-esteem increases your confidence. A woman that has confidence also has self respect. If a woman respects herself, she will also respect others. When a woman builds her self-esteem, she often notices an improvement in her relationships, achievements and happiness in her daily living. Here are some steps to help you build your self-esteem and overcome this issue.

1   Face your fears—(2 Timothy 1:7) *For God hath not given us the spirit of fear; but of power, and of love, and of a sound mind.* Your fears aren't as bad as you think they are. Facing your fears only increases your confidence.

2   Forget your failures—Learn from them and move on. Avoid making the same mistakes again but don't limit yourself by assuming you failed before so you can't succeed this time. Each failure makes you wiser and stronger. Don't be trapped in the past! If you have a deep, dark past full of hurt and pain, look at the

bright side; you're still standing. You may have some scars, bumps and bruises from past hurts, but you're still alive and breathing. What the devil meant for bad, God will work it out for your good.

3   Know what you want and ask for it—You deserve to have your dreams come true. If you believe it, you can achieve it! (Matthew 7:7) *Ask, and it shall be given unto you; seek, and ye shall find; knock and it shall be opened unto you.* Go after what you want. If you want to lose weight, just do it! You should start to walk, exercise, eat healthy and drink plenty of water. If you want that Bachelor's Degree, Master's or Ph.D. just do it! Go to college, take online courses, make it happen. If you want the man of your dreams, go after him. Just be careful because there is a thin line between pursuing and stalking. Laughing! The things you want in life are not going to fall from the sky. You must measure how bad you want them. If you want them bad enough, ask for them. It's time for women to pursue their happiness.

> *Reward yourself when you succeed*—Quit waiting for people to pat you on the back and say, "job well done." Don't expect people to take pride in your accomplishments. It's much better when you do it for yourself.

Only you know the measure of your success. What's important to you may not mean a hill of beans to someone else. You should celebrate your own birthday. You should go out on the town and celebrate your new promotion. Reward yourself!

Talk—Often women with low self-esteem go through life making assumptions. You assume nobody likes you. You assume people are ignoring you or discounting you. You assume people don't want you to be a part of the click. Girlfriend, open your mouth and TALK! Communicate your interests. In order to obtain a friend you must show yourself friendly. Contrary to what you believe, not everybody read minds. You may be a really nice person, but if you never talk to people, they may feel you are shy, private, stuck up or don't want to be bothered. Communication is the key!

Don't be defeated—Try something else. You are not going to be defeated by one failed attempt are you? Most women fail in love a couple of times before we obtain a successful relationship or marriage. I'm sure you've heard the old saying "It's better the second time around." Sometimes all you need is a different approach, different people and different resources. Always remember where there is vision, God makes provision.

Beloved, follow these steps and start building your self-esteem. God's will is that we live well and enjoy life being confident and assertive in our purpose and place in society.

FINANCIAL ISSUES... The lack of money is not your issue. It's you that doesn't manage and budget the money you do have. It's you that lives outside your means. It's you constantly trying to keep up with Joneses. It's you trying to drive a Mercedes and can't afford to keep gas in it. It's you that shops until you drop, buying clothes to dress to impress. It's you that purchases a home that you have to constantly struggle to pay the mortgage. How much fun is that? It's you that has your priorities all screwed up. Don't get me wrong women, if you work, you should enjoy some of the finer things in life. But you need to use common sense, too. If you are buying the things you want but have to borrow money for lunch, gas and bills from your family and friends, it's you that I'm referring to. You don't have financial issues, you are just financially challenged. (Colossians 3:2) Set your affection on things above, not on things on the earth. Everything you buy or invest money into in this life is going to fade away, only what you do for Christ will last. Learn to spend wisely. Establish a budget and stay within it. Learn to save some money for emergencies or unexpected expenses.

SUBMISSIVENESS ISSUES...Being submissive to your husband or significant other is not your issue. It's you that marry men that are not worthy of your submission. Let's look at the definition of submission. It means to yield to another's desires without resistance. Many women today refuse to yield to their spouse's desires without some resistance because of their companion's lack of leadership. Many men in today's society fail to illustrate leadership in their marriages, homes, relationships, careers, finances and personal growth. God created man first and put him over the woman, and his original plan was that the man would be the head. However, somewhere between creation and now, some men have neglected their role as the head, the husband, the provider, and the ruler. It is sad to say but women are partially to blame. Yes, I said it and I mean it…now let's talk about it!

Women, it is important that we marry men that have proven their ability to lead us in every aspect of life meaning spiritually, financially, emotionally and physically. Often women elect to marry men that are not capable of taking care of themselves let alone taking care of a wife, children and household. This creates resistance. I will be the first to admit being submissive was a huge issue with me during my marriage. My ex-husband was a truck driver and changed companies frequently. I found myself carrying the financial burdens of the household. Therefore, I felt I had the right to call the shots and make all the major decisions pertaining to the household because I was winning most of the bread. As I began to examine the situation, a shifting of responsibility had occurred. I was living a spiritual life and he was not, so I constantly challenged his motives for career moves, investments, household purchases, etc. We were both fighting for power and the upper hand. This tug-of-war mentality became fatal for our marriage. He wanted me to step back, yet he refused to step up. He wanted me to submit to his ways, but he refused to commit to God's ways. I'll be the first to admit that when you are saved, walking in the knowledge of God, it is hard to submit to a man that will not commit to Christ. On the other hand, since my divorce, I met an interesting man. To be quite frank, he's very impressive. For the first time in my life, I've been able to relinquish my dominating attitude. I was trying to analyze what made this particular man so different. I've always been attracted to handsome, hard working, charming and educated men. I finally figured it out. I can see that he is a blessed man. I see that he works hard to maintain quality living. Through his hard work, he has achieved financial stability. He is educated, self-disciplined and upholds good family morals. He is very ambitious. He is well rounded, and we are able to converse on any topic. I love all of these qualities which he possesses. However, what I love most about him is the fact that he has proven to me that he is responsible and makes good decisions regarding the welfare of those he loves. Our friendship is still young and under construction. I'm not sure what the future holds for us but I do know that I could easily submit to him or any other man like him that reflects these qualities. Beloved, you don't have a problem being submissive. Your issue is finding the right man that you can trust to have your best interest at heart.

DEPRESSION ISSUES... Depression is not your issue. It's you that doesn't realize you are too blessed to be depressed and stressed. It's you that thrives on the negative in every situation. It's you that feels your life is not worth living. It's you that chooses to stop laughing and smiling. It's you that isolates yourself from the people you love and the people that love you. Women should understand that the effects of depression can impact every aspect of life. Activities you once enjoyed are no longer interesting to you. Even love, an emotion of pleasure, becomes difficult to feel when you are struggling with a spirit of depression. (2 Corinthians 4:8–9) *We are troubled on every side, yet not distressed; we are perplexed, but not in despair; *Persecuted, but not forsaken; cast down, but not destroyed.* Everybody has troubles and trials. All women experience hardship and disappointments. Some women may not admit it, but we have all been dumped by a man that we were head over hills in love with. We all have experienced the loss of loved ones. We all find ourselves in a financial bind from time to time. It's just a part of life! Allow me to share with you a passage of scriptures that I read when I'm depressed, stressed or unmotivated.

¹The earth is the LORD's, and the fulness thereof;

the world, and they that dwell therein. ²For he hath founded it upon the seas, and established it upon the floods. ³Who shall ascend into the hill of the LORD? or who shall stand in his holy place? ⁴He that hath clean hands, and a pure heart; who hath not lifted up his soul unto vanity, nor sworn deceitfully. ⁵He shall receive the blessing from the LORD, and righteousness from the God of his salvation. ⁶This is the generation of them that seek him, that seek thy face, O Jacob. Selah. ⁷Lift up your heads, O ye gates; and be ye lift up, ye everlasting doors; and the King of glory shall come in. ⁸Who is this King of glory? The LORD strong and mighty, the LORD mighty in battle. ⁹Lift up your heads, O ye gates; even lift them up, ye everlasting doors; and the King of glory shall come in. ¹⁰Who is this King of glory? The LORD of hosts, he is the King of glory. Selah.

Psalm 24:1–10

Beloved, when you allow the King of Glory to come in, love, joy, peace and happiness come in also. Stop whining all the time about your situation. Learn to speak life into whatever you are going through. Always remember you are what you speak. If you say you are more than a conqueror, so it is. If you say you are happy, so it is. If you say all is well with my soul, so it is. Think positive! Speak positive things about yourself and others. Hold your head up! Put a smile on your face. Learn to laugh and enjoy your everyday life.

BATTERING ISSUES... This issue is somewhat touchy! Your issue is not being with an abusive man. It's your way of thinking that lures you to stay with someone that abuses you. In ministering to battered women, I see the same pattern of thinking. Battered women think they have to stick by their man no matter what. They are ashamed of their husband's or significant other's behavior. Therefore, they feel compelled to keep the abuse private. Some women think they can't make it alone. Some women are very understanding about the abuse. They honestly think maybe he'll change or maybe it was something they did to provoke his behavior. Battered women stay in abusive relationships out of fear. There are so many facts that all women should know about battering. Battering is the behavior used to establish power and control over another person through fear and intimidation, often including the threat or use of violence. Battering happens when one person believes they are entitled to control another. Assault, battering and domestic violence are all crimes. God has a purpose and plan for your life, and, trust me, it is not for you to be hurt and abused. Beloved, if you are a victim of physical, sexual or psychological abuse, you don't deserve it.

I rejoice in the Lord that I have never been a victim of battering. I have been blessed to date intelligent men that understand my capabilities. I am capable of being a wife, a minister, a queen, a virtuous woman, a help-mate, a confidant and a friend. However, I am not and will never be capable of being any man's punching bag, doormat or foot stool. It is important to establish this understanding early in a relationship. Being a single woman now, before I agree to go on a date, I lay the ground rules upfront: I don't hit men and men don't hit me, I don't curse men and men don't curse me, I don't embarrass men and men don't embarrass men, I don't control men and men don't control me. I advise them of the true fact that I'm still a work in progress and in the event you forget any of our ground rules, I will not turn the other cheek. Certainly not! Don't you dare let my collar, my calling or my finesse fool you; I still have some thuggish tendencies that will resurface when provoked. Laughing! Seriously, I have feelings, morals and standards. I told you that I keep it real, I may not get into a physical brawl, but I would definitely get the law officials involved. Can you say "charges," "right to remain silent?"

Okay, I got real emotional for a moment. The very thought of a man abusing me or any other woman disturbs me. Again, I'm so thankful that I've never been a victim of abuse. However, I found some information that could be beneficial for women that might be reading this book that are battered victims.

Safety Plan Tips…

- During an argument, or if you feel tension building, avoid areas in your home where weapons might be available—the kitchen, bathroom, bedroom or workshops.

- If there are weapons in your household such as firearms, lock them up!

- Know where there is a safe exit from your home—a window, elevator or stairwell.

- Discuss the situation with a trusted neighbor if you can. Ask them to call 911 if they hear a disturbance. Find a code word to use with them if you need the police.

- Always keep a packed bag ready.

- Know where you would go to be safe if you have to leave, even if you don't really think you need to.

These are great safety plan tips. I would also like to share a passage of scripture that will encourage the hearts of any woman especially those that are victims of battering.

> [1]*The LORD is my light and my salvation; whom shall I fear? the LORD is the strength of my life; of whom shall I be afraid?* [2]*When the wicked, even mine enemies and my foes, came upon me to eat up my flesh, they stumbled and fell.* [3]*Though an host should encamp against me, my heart shall not fear: though war should rise against me, in this will I be confident.* [4]*One thing have I desired of the LORD, that will I seek after; that I may dwell in the house of the LORD all the days of my life, to behold the beauty of the LORD, and to enquire in his temple.* [5]*For in the time of trouble he shall hide me in his pavilion: in the secret of his tabernacle shall he hide me; he shall*

set me up upon a rock. ⁶And now shall mine head be lifted up above mine enemies round about me: therefore will I offer in his tabernacle sacrifices of joy; I will sing, yea, I will sing praises unto the LORD. ⁷Hear, O LORD, when I cry with my voice: have mercy also upon me, and answer me. ⁸When thou saidst, Seek ye my face; my heart said unto thee, Thy face, LORD, will I seek. ⁹Hide not thy face far from me; put not thy servant away in anger: thou hast been my help; leave me not, neither forsake me, O God of my salvation. ¹⁰When my father and my mother forsake me, then the LORD will take me up. ¹¹Teach me thy way, O LORD, and lead me in a plain path, because of mine enemies. ¹²Deliver me not over unto the will of mine enemies: for false witnesses are risen up against me, and such as breathe out cruelty. ¹³I had fainted, unless I had believed to see the goodness of the LORD in the land of the living. ¹⁴Wait on the LORD: be of good courage, and he shall strengthen thine heart: wait, I say, on the LORD.

Psalm 27:1–14

Learn this passage of scriptures. Memorize it! Receive

it into your spirit and watch God deliver you from the hands of your enemies.

DESPERATION ISSUES...Women, why do we act so desperate? My heart goes out to desperate women because we don't even see how bad our issues are. Trust me on this one... it's you! I observe women that are so desperate for a mate that they will accept anything from anybody. I see smart, beautiful, educated and successful women walking around with dead beat companions. The real issue is you being controlled by a spirit of neediness. Desperate women have a tendency to be needy! They desperately need a mate, and they desperately need their mate to need them. Women that live in a state of desperation compromise their standards, beliefs, ethics and morals just to feed into their needy spirit. I minister to some women that are successful and hardworking but they date losers! They are involved with unemployed men, men with drug addictions and men that don't have their own form of transportation. Some of these men still live at home with their mothers or sisters. This is typical behavior of a desperate woman. She has worked hard to achieve her goals and yet she entertains men that have no goals at all. She will give so much and receive so little in return. Don't get me wrong, I do not encourage women to be gold diggers. However, I think every relationship should be well balanced. The relationship should consist of giving and taking. If a woman does all the giving, all the bending and all the compromising to maintain her mate's affection while he gives her nothing in return sounds like a desperate woman to me. I'm not saying that a man has to spend a ton of money on you or has to be rich for you to show interest in him. I'm simply saying it helps when your man is in a position to take care of himself and do a little something for you from time to time. I offended a young man once because I said, "A man must have a J.O.B. if he wants to holler at me." He said there are a lot of good unemployed men that are capable of loving a woman. I told him this might be true, but as for me and my house, we are going to work! Don't get me wrong, this doesn't mean I want a man to take care of me. This simply means I will not take care of a man that is not responsible enough to take care of himself. Sorry, I'm just not that desperate. Perhaps you are reading and thinking, "How do I know whether or not I'm desperate?" Here are a few hints to help you identify your desperation status:

If you allow every man you date to move into your

home RENT FREE, this is a sign that you are desperate! Don't try to tell me that he didn't have anywhere else to live. Where was he living before he met you?

If you become a banking institution for your mate, this is a sign that you are desperate. I'm not saying you can't buy him dinner sometime or do a good deed for him from time to time. I'm not saying you can't buy your man a nice gift or two. However, I'm saying when you start including his bills in your monthly budget, you are desperate. When you start spending your hard earned money to support your man's habits, you are desperate. When you are constantly loaning your man money and he never repays you, you are desperate. Let's be real for a moment, if a man has to borrow money from you it means he doesn't have any of his own. What makes you think he'll pay you back? Let me guess, because he said he would. Yeah right! I see women on TV courts every day filing judgments against their former boyfriends. They try to retrieve the monies that they loaned during the relationships. Many of them walk away sorrowfully because the judge views it as gifts. Many of these men consider them as gifts also. They might ask to borrow money but somewhere between them borrowing and you giving, it becomes a gift in their mind. Why?... because they feel you are just that desperate that you will not know the difference between a loan and a gift. Many women co-sign for cars, motorcycles, credit cards and electronics. The judge will ask, "Why did you do all this?" They all have the same stupid answers: "I thought he loved me," "I was just trying to help him get on his feet," "He was supposed to get a job and pay me back." Think, women! Any man that loves you will see you as a woman not as a bank. If you are constantly giving favors to your mate, the issue is not your mate. It's you being desperate.

If you have to change for every man you date, this is another sign that you are desperate. Be yourself. You can't change your colors for every man you meet. One man wants you to be thin. The other one wants you thick. One man wants your hair long, and the other one likes it short. Women, define who you are and whose you are. You are the most precious vessel to ever walk the earth and if your man can't accept you and respect you for who you are then let him walk. Men are like city buses, one comes along every ten minutes.

Beloved, we can't be so desperate that we compromise our goals, standards, beliefs and morals. Take time to look for balance in the relationship. I know sometimes it seems as if all men are in the same boat. Therefore, the easy the thing to do is to take one and work with him. Certainly not! All men are not in the same boat. Some men are in canoes; they are just fishing to having a good time at somebody else's expense. Some men are in sailboats; they need a good woman to help guide them in the right direction. Some men are in yachts; they are private, sophisticated and want to cruise with the woman of their dreams. Contrary to what most women believe, there are still some good, employed, intellectual and attractive men searching for their missing rib. The problem with women in today's society is that we are so desperate and busy trying to find balance in unequally yoked relationships that we overlook the men that are most compatible with us and our needs. Quit being desperate! Don't lower your standards just for the sake of having a man. I had a young lady tell me that she would rather have a piece of a man than to have no man at all. My response was "I'd rather wait on a hero, than to waste time on a zero."

MESS STARTING & MESS DWELLING ISSUES...

Your name being in a mess is not your issue. It's you starting and dwelling in messy situations. I hear women saying, "I'm tired of my name being in a mess." It is absolutely nothing wrong with your name. The problem is your mouth. (James 3:8) *But the tongue can no man tame; it is an unruly evil, full of deadly poison.* So true! Women talk too much. We have to bring everything out in the open. "Girl, did you see that?" "Have you heard about this?" "What do you think about them?" "I could be wrong but…" All of these are typical ice breakers for women with mess starting and mess dwelling issues. However, some women are more spiritual with their messy behavior. They say things like, "God told me to tell you," or "the Lord placed it in my spirit" or "God showed me." You have to be aware of women that are always telling you what God told them to tell you. I find in my walk with Christ that the majority of the things that God tells me are for me about me. Some of my best sermons were for me and my life. I have made many enemies because of four little words I often use: "I DON'T RECEIVE IT." You should get familiar with those words also. When people began telling me mess about other people's business, I tell them, "I DON'T RECEIVE IT." I have my own issues, my own problems, my own challenges; I don't want to be involved in the church gossip, community mess, workplace saga. "I DON'T RECEIVE IT." We are women not trash collectors. Therefore, we must stop dealing with garbage, junk and mess. There is work to be done in the building of God's kingdom. There is no time for foolishness, gossiping, backbiting and digging ditches. Beloved, my desire is that we all survive as the body of Christ. The only way we can survive is to love and encourage each other. When we eliminate the mess, we will see God begin to bless. I pray that every woman reading this book will become a certified M.B. (Mess Buster). Whether it is church mess, work mess, home mess or family mess, stop dwelling in it. Discourage people from bringing mess to your attention, and you discourage yourself from taking mess to others. It is really sad to see grown women acting like elementary girls with "she said that I said that they said we said." Please spare me! Grow up! Stop being so messy! Mind your own business! Stay focused on the things of God!

As women in today's society, we struggle with so many issues. The list goes on and on. Some of us have health issues, weight issues, holiness issues, career issues, dead beat daddy issues, etc. Whatever you classify as your issue, I'm certain that if you examine it closely, you'll find that your issue is you.

GETTING IN THE FACE OF JESUS

For she said, if I may touch but his clothes, I shall be whole.

Mark 5:28

Somewhere between creation and now, we have misconstrued salvation. Many women feel because of issues, problems, past mistakes, disappointments, failures, reputations and lifestyles, we are disqualified from making contact with Jesus. Certainly not! Most of the women in the New Testament that Jesus touched were women with dirty issues. Some had tainted reputations. Some were adulterous women. Some had troubled children. Nevertheless, they knew that deliverance was available to them; it was just a matter of getting in the face of Jesus. (John 3:17) *For God sent not his Son into the world to condemn the world: but that the world through him might be saved.* For this reason alone, we are worthy of getting in the face of Jesus. Through Christ all women can be touched, healed, delivered and set free from any issues. We must stop thinking that our issues are too bad, too dirty and too overwhelming for God to handle. Abraham asked the question, "Is there anything too hard for God?" Allow me to answer that... Certainly not! Women don't have any issues, problems addictions, habits or hang-ups that God can't work out, change or correct. It's just a matter of getting in the face of Jesus.

Many women go to church and sit in the very back pew to avoid drawing attention to themselves and their issues. Some women sit quietly hoping that the pastor will preach a message, the choir will sing a song or perhaps somebody will pray the right prayer and boom... shazaam... instant deliverance from our issues. Certainly not! True deliverance does not come by touching Jesus through the men and women of God. It goes far beyond that. We must make personal contact with Jesus before seeing changes in our lives and our issues. I love NBA basketball. I think it's the best thing since popsicles. I know of many great players. Michael Jordan, Larry Bird and Magic Johnson are all legends. However, calling one of them to chit chat on the phone or to ask for a favor would be a terrible waste of my time. Reason being, I do not have a personal relationship with them. I only know of them. So it is with Jesus. Too many women today only know of him, and the reason he doesn't respond to our call is because we have not established an up close and personal relationship with him. We know of him based on what we see on television. Or perhaps what he has done for others. Well, I have bad news and some good news for women today. The bad news is that you can't get delivered through your Madear and Grandpa's relationship with God. I understand your parents are spirit filled and you are surrounded by saved friends and co-workers that are daily walking in the light, but you must personally get in the face of Jesus for yourself. Here's the good news, Jesus is waiting to establish a personal relationship with you. He's desires to know you! Many women today really desire deliverance from their issues but they haven't made any contact with the "Deliverer." Some women stand in need of financial provisions but have never made contact with the "Provider." Some women are waiting for yokes to be destroyed and shackles to be broken but haven't made any personal contact with the "Chain Breaker." Women, your relationship with Christ must be personal. (Matthew 6:33) *But seek ye first the kingdom of God, and his righteousness; and all these things shall be added unto you.* The key to deliverance is to seek him; get in the face of Jesus. Press your way into his presence. In spite of the issues, circumstances and conditions, we must keep pressing for the blessing. Our healing, deliverance and breakthroughs are all found in the presence of the Lord.

Perhaps right now you are thinking to yourself, "How do I get in the face of Jesus?" Well, it's a process. Allow me to explain.

> [9]*That if thou shalt confess with thy mouth the Lord Jesus, and shalt believe in thine heart that God hath raised him from the dead, thou shalt be saved.* [10]*For with the heart man believeth unto righteousness; and with the mouth confession is made unto salvation.*

> Romans 10:9–10

Confessing with your mouth and believing in your heart are the first steps to getting in the face of Jesus and making contact. Nevertheless, there is another important step that women constantly overlook.

> *But ye shall receive power, after the Holy Ghost is come upon you: and ye shall be witnesses unto me both in Jerusalem, and in all Judaea, and in Samaria, and unto the uttermost part of the earth.*

> Acts 1:8

This is the missing piece of the puzzle. We must be filled with the Holy Ghost. This is how we make personal contact with Jesus. Earlier in my walk with Christ, I attended church on a regular basis. I maintained positions within the church. I attended Sunday school regularly. However, I was still struggling with the same old issues. I kept falling for the same old tricks of the enemy. I continued to make the same stupid decisions. It wasn't until I was filled with the Holy Spirit that I saw the manifestation of God in my life. Many women today are stuck where I used to be. They have mastered the easy part of confessing with the mouth and believing with the heart but have not been filled with the Holy Ghost. My pastor sums it up better than anybody I've ever heard. He once stated: "In the Old Testament, God was for us! In the New Testament, God was with us! After the death and resurrection of Jesus, God sent the Holy Spirit to get in us!" That's where the personal contact comes into play. Once the Holy Spirit is received in us, we then receive power to live victoriously in Christ. Imagine trying to drive a brand new convertible without any fuel. Although the car is new and shiny and has potential to go, there must be fuel in the tank to make sure the car takes off and perform. So it is with believers today, when we confess with the mouth and believe in our heart, we become individuals with the potential of living a saved life, but we must be baptized in the Holy Spirit to obtain power to take off and perform holiness in our walk with Christ.

The scriptures indicate that the certain woman touched Jesus' garment. Jesus then turned to the crowd and asked, "Who touched me?" The certain woman had to identify herself. As women today, we must identify ourselves to Jesus. We must confess to him our issues and show him that we have the faith and trust him to have the power to loose us from the things that are not beneficial to our walk with him. Often, women try to steer clear of getting in the face of Jesus and identifying who we are in him because we fear the consequences and convictions that come from being in the Lord's presence. When you go face to face with Jesus and receive the Holy Spirit, responsibility follows. You can't live the same sinful life and be at peace. You will find it difficult to keep struggling with the same old issues. You will not keep falling for Satan's tired old tricks and tactics. You will want to do wrong and can't, simply because of your acquaintance with Jesus.

There were several times in my life when people said and did hurtful things to me and I had plotted to retaliate. Girlfriend, I was going to give the perpetrators a piece of my mind. I was determined to voice my concerns. Notice, this is what "I said" and what "I planned" and what "I decided." Nevertheless, because of my acquaintance with Jesus, when I saw those people that had persecuted me and scandalized my name, I embraced them in love and never said a word. Do you know how hard it is to love somebody that hates your guts? Do you know how tough it is to be cordial with someone that digs ditches for you? It is very hard! I tried to figure out what happened to my original plan. Notice the key words are "my original plan of retaliation." At first I thought I was losing my mind. Then I thought I must be a chicken. Then I thought maybe I just couldn't come up with the right words to tell them. I then realized that nothing is wrong with me. This is typical behavior of a woman that has been touched by God. I am filled with the Holy Spirit. One day I got in the face of Jesus and with one touch, my life was changed forever.

All women that have been touched by Jesus can witness to the fact you can achieve things you never thought you could do such as doing good to people that spitefully misuse you. You can pray for people that talk about you. You can speak life and blessing in the lives of people that have spoken death and curses in your life. You can love people that you know hate you. Let's go a step further. Some women can shout for joy in the midst of a crisis. Some women can even smile and laugh in midst of their heartache and pain. When you are touched by Jesus, you will stop thinking in the natural and start thinking in the supernatural. You will stop walking in the flesh and start running in the spirit. These are typical results of getting in the face of Jesus and being filled with his Holy Spirit.

Women, we can no longer function with the mind-set that we are unworthy to get in the face of Jesus. Today would be a good day for you to rebuke the devil and his plan to sift you of your deliverance. Find you a secret place and get in the face of Jesus. It's no secret anymore. We have established that all women have issues. However, we need to understand that these issues can be annihilated with one touch from Jesus. (Romans 8:37) *Nay, in all these things we are more than conquerors through him that loved us.* Whatever the issue is, you are a conqueror through Christ. Don't allow the devil to deceive you and make you think your issues and your problems are too much for God to handle. I speak from experience when I say getting in the face of Jesus gives him the opportunity to fix what is broken in you. Jesus specializes in bringing ease to troubled minds, healing wounded spirits, lifting up bowed down heads and saving sin sick souls; he's just waiting on you to make your move into his presence.

I admired this certain woman with an issue for getting in the face of Jesus. It wasn't easy for her. It was a large crowd of people that she had to get around, but the Bible said that she pressed her way through the crowd of people. Sometimes the reason women can't make it into the presence of the Lord is because they are stuck in the crowd. You are pressing for the blessing but you can't seem to get beyond people; therefore, you're just stuck! You seem to have the same problems with the same people. There is no growth in your spirituality. Many women are stuck in dead end relationships and marriages. Some women are stuck in financial ruts and mediocre jobs. Some women are stuck in negative friendships. Here's another "is you." The reason you are stuck is you refuse to think outside of the box. I talk to women on a daily basis that have a narrow way of thinking. Some women believe they've been stuck so long that they can't be delivered and set free from their issues. They really believe in their minds that this is as good as it gets. Beloved, until you change your mindset and your negative way of thinking, you will never move or improve your standard of living. You'll just remain stuck in the crowd. You simply become a "No Woman." No deliverance! No change! No breakthrough! No hope! No joy! No peace! No Jesus! I beseech you today that you get unstuck and keep pressing for your blessings. Regardless of your issues, your problems, your troubles, your circumstances and people, press your way into the presence of Jesus and identify yourself; you will see great things begin to unfold in your life. Healing, deliverance, breakthroughs, miracles and salvation are all found in the presence of Jesus.

> [10]*And he was teaching in one of the synagogues on the sabbath.* [11]*And, behold, there was a woman which had a spirit of infirmity eighteen years, and was bowed together, and could in no wise lift up herself.* [12]*And when Jesus saw her, he called her to him, and said unto her, Woman, thou art loosed from thine infirmity.* [13]*And he laid his hands on her: and immediately she was made straight, and glorified God.*

> Luke 13:10–13

This woman had been struggling with the issue of being bent over for eighteen years but when she got in the presence of Jesus, he laid hands on her and immediately she was made straight. Once again, an issue was no longer an issue. Notice this certain woman wasn't looking for deliverance! Deliverance was looking for her simply because she was in the presence of Jesus. The scripture states that Jesus saw her and called her to him. I believe in my heart that if women would just get closer to Jesus, the deliverance that you can't seem to find will soon find you. Too many women are walking around bent over. We are bent over physically, mentally, spiritually, emotionally and financially, but here's the good news. Just as Jesus loosed this woman from her infirmities and straightened her out, we too can be loosed and set free. It is just a matter of us approaching Jesus boldly with water-walking faith knowing that he has the power to do a new thing in us. (Ephesians 3:20) *Now unto him that is able to do exceeding abundantly above all that we ask or think, according to the power that worketh in us.* I consider all women to be a work in progress. Getting in the face of Jesus allows God to mold and shape us into the woman God has carefully created us to be.

I devoted my life to Christ at age eight. However, I didn't get in the face of Jesus until age thirty-two, and my life has not been the same. When I got in the face of Jesus and identified myself, I told the Lord that I was a wretch undone. I was a "certain woman with issues."

I confessed to Jesus that I had not done everything by the good book. I told God that I wanted to present my body as a living sacrifice holy and acceptable unto him, and immediately he touched my heart, my mind and my soul. Immediately, he began to purge me and prune me of the things that were not like him. It was like a Holy Ghost takeover. God's presence began to invade my spirit. I didn't know what God was going to do in me or through me, but I could see him preparing me for something greater in him. God chose me to evangelize. Notice I said God chose me. He tried calling me but I didn't answer. I tried to run just like Jonah tried to run, but God caught me just as he caught Jonah. God chose me to motivate his people with the gospel of Jesus Christ. He instructed me to feed his sheep. I was obedient and accepted the evangelism ministry that God had planted within me and the rest is history.

My life is continuing to soar to new heights. I'm blessed beyond blessed. I walk in great favor! I'm single, saved and satisfied! I have more now than I could have ever imagined. God has given me double for all my trouble. It didn't come easy! I had to get in the face of Jesus. (John 4:24) *God is a spirit and they that worship him, must worship him in spirit and in truth.* I stopped being religious and started being spiritual. Now, I have established a personal spiritual relationship with God. We have a very unique relationship. I know God, and God knows me. I recognize God's voice, and he recognizes my every cry. I strive to please God, and he strives to reward me. God knows what my future holds, and I know he holds my future. God knows what I want, and I'm thankful that he supplies my needs. This beautiful relationship was developed as the outcome of me getting in the face of Jesus!

And he said unto her, Daughter, thy faith hath made thee whole; go in peace, and be whole of thy plague.

Mark 5:34

Go in peace! Often, women are healed, delivered and set free from issues but can't live in peace. We have enough faith to be delivered but have no power to live in peace after deliverance. Many women in today's society beat themselves over the head regarding issues in which they have already been delivered and set free. It is not others that remind us of our past issues, it is us reminding ourselves. Throughout the New Testament when Jesus healed and delivered people, he instructed them to "go in peace." I feel when Jesus spoke the words "go in peace." It was his unique way of saying, you're free, you're delivered, I forgive you, it is finished, move on and live better. It was not Jesus' desire to save us and still maintain the same quality of living. Just as Jesus' healing and deliverance brought new life, hope and freedom to the people in biblical days; his healing and deliverance should also bring new life, hope and freedom to us today. (John 14:27) *Peace I leave with you, my peace I give unto you: not as the world giveth, give I unto you. Let not your heart be troubled, neither let it be afraid.*

Stop dwelling on past issues, mistakes, hurts, disappointments and shortcomings that you have already been delivered from. It is time for us to live in peace. What's done is done! The sole purpose of being delivered from our issues is to be free, at peace and enjoying the greater things of God. I once heard a song say, "free your mind and the rest will follow." Many women today are unable to live in peace because they are delivered spiritually but their mind is still harboring the thought of the issue. Allow me to explain.

After I was delivered from my divorce issues, I found myself treating the word "marriage" like an infectious disease. Although I was over the marriage itself and the love for the ex-husband had been put in perspective order, the thought of me getting re-married made me sick at the stomach. Yes, I was okay with the divorce. Yes, I had grieved, forgiven and let it go! Yes, I had moved on with my life, but the very thought of remarrying would make my blood pressure shoot through the roof. I avoided every man that mentioned to me their intentions of getting married. I finally realized that I was delivered spiritually but not mentally. I had to make up in my mind that marriage is not a bad thing. Marriage is the right concept, but sometimes we marry the wrong person. As a result, the marriage ends in divorce. However, the fact still remains the same; marriage is honorable in the sight of the Lord. My view on marriage is different now. The thought of me marrying the man that God has carefully chosen and ordained for me makes me smile. The thought of being joined in holy matrimony with a man that loves me like God loves the church gives me goose bumps. I'm free from my divorce issues spiritually and mentally. When giving my marital status, I tell people that I'm happily divorced! Meaning I'm at peace! We can't afford to entertain negative thoughts regarding deliverance from things in our past because if you let your thoughts ride, they will take over and drive. Your thoughts will become words, your words will become actions, your actions will become habits and your habits will become character.

Looking at the word peace, Webster defines peace as 1) a state of tranquility or quiet 2) freedom from disquieting or oppressive thoughts or emotions 3) harmony in personal relations. Peace is what every woman should possess in today's society. There are so many benefits to living in peace. Living in peace allows us to keep our mind stayed on God's perfect plan for our life. Living in peace allows us to better recognize and understand the movement of God within the body of Christ. Living in peace also permits us to hear from God and receive what he speaks directly into our life and our situation. Satan despises those who live in peace. Therefore, immediately after a person gets saved, delivered and set free from their issues, all hell breaks loose in his or her life. Satan will attempt to use anybody, anytime, anywhere, anyhow and any situation to cause havoc and confusion in your daily living. He recognizes that a person who possesses the peace of God will not be easily shaken by his tricks, traps, strategies and distractions. Therefore, Satan often causes us to stumble by using the same old tricks. He attacks our finances, romances, family affairs and our health. Satan knows that when he distracts us with financial setbacks, broken marriages, sinking relationships, rebellious children, negative friends, job downsizing, family feuds, tragedies and deaths, he has us exactly where he wants us, unfocused. How long will we allow Satan and his tricks to take our eyes off the prize? Satan came to steal, kill and destroy, but Jesus came that we might have life and have it more abundantly. We must find refuge in knowing that Jesus wants us to live in peace. Whether good, bad, happy or sad times, we must maintain our peace. We must possess peace in our heart, mind and spirit. We must learn to trust God to keep us and work all things out for our good.

My most intimate time with God is between the hours of 3:00 and 5:00 A.M. I'm able to commune with God in a quiet, peaceful and calm environment. Please, don't think God's presence is so much more overwhelming in the early morning hours than any other time of the day. Personally, I feel because there are no distractions around me like whining children, a ringing phone, unexpected company or a blasting radio or television, early morning is the most peaceful time for me to worship and fellowship with God. All women should have a designated time to commune with God and give him your undivided attention. Communion allows us to speak to God and listen to what God is speaking to us. Communion is also a time for us to receive instructions, correction and revelation. Satan despises this type of peaceful communion with God and plots to keep us from having these daily worship experiences. It is certain that when you are spending intimate time with God, your problems and issues become minor. Personally, I've had issues that I struggled with that seemed as large as giants, but once I began to commune with God, the problems began to look more like grasshoppers. It is so important to women to maintain a good intimate relationship with God. I feel this is why God is so fond of marriage because this is an example of the type of intimacy that he desires to share with us. He wants us to unite with him and spend quality time with him and his Word. Just as intimacy strengthens your marriage, it also strengthens your relationship with God.

Do you really believe Satan is going to let you live in peace without a fight? Certainly not! This explains why Satan comes in like a flood the minute a person confesses Jesus as their Lord and Savior. He attacks the marriage, the children, health and wealth. He will even strike in the family, neighborhood, community, city and country. He uses drama, trauma, death, disaster and tragedies to draw our attention away from God. Satan takes great pleasure in watching us lay awake at night worrying about things we have no control over. He is so proud when we get so busy stressing that we overlook the many blessings God grants us from day to day. As a matter of fact, Satan laughs when we fret about cheating husbands, uncommitted lovers, broken friendships, church mess, delinquent bills, sickness and other things that keep us in bondage. Women, we have allowed the devil to get too much satisfaction from our failure to live in peace. Living in today's society, peace is a necessity for our survival.

Beloved, I admonish you to live in peace, regardless of the distractions, set ups and the set backs that are happening in your life. Keep your eyes on the prize! Don't allow yourself to keep looking back on your old issues and used tos.

> [5]And it was told the king of Egypt that the people fled: and the heart of Pharaoh and of his servants was turned against the people, and they said, Why have we done this, that we have let Israel go from serving us? [6]And he made ready his chariot, and took his people with him: [7]And he took six hundred chosen chariots, and all the chariots of Egypt, and captains over every one of them. [8]And the LORD hardened the heart of Pharaoh king of Egypt, and he pursued after the children of Israel: and the children of Israel went out with an high hand. [9]But the Egyptians pursued after

them, all the horses and chariots of Pharaoh, and his horsemen, and his army, and overtook them encamping by the sea, beside Pihahiroth, before Baalzephon. ¹⁰And when Pharaoh drew nigh, the children of Israel lifted up their eyes, and, behold, the Egyptians marched after them; and they were sore afraid: and the children of Israel cried out unto the LORD. ¹¹And they said unto Moses, Because there were no graves in Egypt, hast thou taken us away to die in the wilderness? wherefore hast thou dealt thus with us, to carry us forth out of Egypt? ¹²Is not this the word that we did tell thee in Egypt, saying, Let us alone, that we may serve the Egyptians? For it had been better for us to serve the Egyptians, than that we should die in the wilderness.

Exodus 14:5–12

Women have this same mindset today. Once we get delivered and the first sign of trouble comes our way, the first response is to turn back and return to what we are used to. Many of us go back to areas in our lives that we are familiar with. Instead of living in peace and facing the obstacles, we find peace in returning to our past, no matter how dreadful it may be. We return to former issues, lovers, habits, negative friends and hang out spots simply because it was once normal for us. (2 Corinthians 5:17) *Therefore if any man be in Christ, he is a new creature: old things are passed away; behold, all things are become new.* If you were seeking deliverance from people, places and things in your past, that is confirmation that there's nothing there worth returning to. The children of Israel knew there was nothing in Egypt for them but destruction, oppression and misery, but because of their spirit of complacency, their first thought was to go back. I heard the lyrics of a rap song say, "Lean Back, Lean Back." Certainly not! If you would just keep it real for a moment, you'd know there's nothing back there to lean on. Nothing but destruction, oppression, confusion, issues and misery. Who wants to lean back on that? Not me! I'm convinced that my future in God's hands is far greater than anything in my past. My past is full of mistakes, disappointments and sin, but my future is full of God's blessings, favor and promises. Women, we must understand that the primary purpose of being delivered and set free is to come out of the old things and move into the new things that God has stored up for us that are called according to his purpose. Be encouraged and know (John 8:36) *If the Son therefore shall make you free, ye shall be free indeed.*

You are free to live in peace. If a woman lives in bondage after deliverance it is by choice. Personally, I choose to live in peace. We all have a right to live in peace; our faith in God has made us whole in every aspect of life.

When I got saved, delivered and set free for real, I knew that I walking in a strong anointing because immediately I suffered from some of Satan's attacks. I received some knock out punches. I was hit with some blinding blows. My marriage ended in divorce. My calling as an evangelist was challenged because of my gender. My son's grades began to slip, and his behavior began to shift at home and in school. My finances were stretched to the limits. I had two deaths in my family within a three month period. I was desperately trying to adjust to being a single parent after fourteen years of marriage. In the midst of all of these adversities, God blessed me to record my first gospel CD project titled *God Will Deliver.* I was traveling near and far preaching and singing the gospel of Jesus Christ in worship services, programs, conferences, workshops and concerts. Through it all, God kept my mind and heart stayed on him. It wasn't easy, but I was able to sustain the peace of God. The devil thought he was setting me back to fail, but God was setting me up to succeed. Oh yeah, the devil planned for me to be destroyed, but God planned for me to be restored! Who couldn't serve a God like this? I didn't know how things were going to unfold, but I knew God would do the unfolding. Therefore, I found peace in trusting God. I made up in my mind that I would serve God unconditionally. In spite of my issues, circumstances, set ups and set backs, I was determined to please Jesus. My concern was to please God and seek the things of Him. I didn't focus on what I considered to be losses. I didn't dwell on my hurt and weariness. I didn't get worked up about my finances. I just continued to be about my Father's business.

> [37]*And, behold, a woman in the city, which was a sinner, when she knew that Jesus sat at meat in the Pharisee's house, brought an alabaster box of ointment,* [38]*And stood at his feet behind him weeping, and began to wash his feet with tears, and did wipe them with the hairs of her head, and kissed his feet, and anointed them with the ointment.* [39]*Now when the Pharisee which had bidden him saw it, he spake within himself, saying, This man, if he were a prophet, would have known who and what manner of woman this is that toucheth him: for she is a sinner.* [40]*And Jesus answering said unto him, Simon, I have*

somewhat to say unto thee. And he saith, Master, say on. ⁴¹There was a certain creditor which had two debtors: the one owed five hundred pence, and the other fifty. ⁴²And when they had nothing to pay, he frankly forgave them both. Tell me therefore, which of them will love him most? ⁴³Simon answered and said, I suppose that he, to whom he forgave most. And he said unto him, Thou hast rightly judged. ⁴⁴And he turned to the woman, and said unto Simon, Seest thou this woman? I entered into thine house, thou gavest me no water for my feet: but she hath washed my feet with tears, and wiped them with the hairs of her head. ⁴⁵Thou gavest me no kiss: but this woman since the time I came in hath not ceased to kiss my feet. ⁴⁶My head with oil thou didst not anoint: but this woman hath anointed my feet with ointment. ⁴⁷Wherefore I say unto thee, Her sins, which are many, are forgiven; for she loved much: but to whom little is forgiven, the same loveth little. ⁴⁸And he said unto her, Thy sins are forgiven.

Luke 7:37–48

Although she was a certain woman with issues, she

had found sweet peace in Jesus. She was not concerned about her former issues of prostitution and promiscuity. She didn't care about the Pharisees' and the disciples' malicious remarks about her sinful past. She did not focus on the value of the expensive ointment that she used to anoint Jesus' feet. She paid no attention to what was going on around her. She found peace in serving at the feet of Jesus. She sustained her peace by focusing on the things that were pleasing to him. We too must make pleasing Jesus our first priority.

> [33]*But seek ye first the kingdom of God, and his righteousness; and all these things shall be added unto you.* [34]*Take therefore no thought for the morrow: for the morrow shall take thought for the things of itself.*
>
> Matthew 6:33–34

When you begin to seek the kingdom of God first and God's righteousness, everything will fall into place. Your issues that you are struggling with will dissolve because you will better understand that it is not about you but your life is all about Jesus. Our praise, worship and being should glorify God, edify God's people and horrify the devil in hell. I am continuing to live in peace knowing that I am a living witness of a purpose driven life. Each day I strive to show proof that I know God; so that those who don't know God will want to know God simply because they know me. This is true peace.

As you come to the end of this book, I pray that you have witnessed something that pricked your heart and compelled you to confront and overcome your many issues. (Hebrews 12:1) *Wherefore seeing we also are compassed about with so great a cloud of witnesses, let us lay aside every weight, and the sin which doth so easily beset us, and let us run with patience the race that is set before us.* Beloved, we must understand that weight is anything and anybody that holds us down and holds us back. We are living in perilous times, and we don't need the extra weight of our issues holding us down. It is time to drop it off! Whether your issues are loneliness, depression, low self-esteem, no self-esteem, singleness, marital, divorce, rape, molestation, greed, jealousy, stinking thinking, fornication, adultery, negative friends, battering, gold digging, promiscuity, mess starting, gossiping, lying tongue, health, wealth, holiness, baby mama drama, dead end jobs, these issues have weighed you down far too long. All of theses issues keep us separated from God which makes it impossible to connect with his will for our life. It is time we break free and declare victory in Jesus. Women will always be a certain woman, but we don't always have to struggle with the same issues. Deliverance is only one touch away!

ABOUT THE AUTHOR

*G*rowing up in Covington, Tennessee, Rhonda had many childhood dreams and ambitions. Her biggest dream was to grow up and become a world renowned news reporter. Never in a million years did she imagine becoming an author, evangelist or gospel artist. In a sense, you can say her dream still came true because she boldly spreads the good news. Instead of spreading gossip, she spreads the gospel. Whether singing, preaching or writing, she tells of the goodness of our Lord and Savior, Jesus Christ.

Rhonda discovered her gift of singing at a very early age in the church. Later in life she accepted her calling into the ministry of evangelism, exercising her ability and anointing to preach and teach the true and living Word of God. Just when she thought she had reached the pinnacle of her destiny, she discovered her gift of writing. She feels that writing books is the perfect example of God enlarging her territory of ministry.

A Woman and Her Issues is her first book, but she declares that it will not be her last. She's very excited about publishing more books in the near future. She's confident that her books will bless, inspire and encourage everyone that reads them.

Being a young woman, Rhonda walks in many different roles: author, evangelist and gospel artist just to name a few. However, her most important role is being a mother. Although she's passionate about ministry, her first ministry is her son, Tyler. She feels that there is no greater joy than being a mother to a child that understands, adores and honors her spiritual gifts. Her second ministry is her family and her friends. Her leisure time is sometimes challenged. However, she always finds time to enjoy those that are very dear to her heart.

Rhonda is an ordained minister. She serves at Greater Imani Church and Christian Center in Memphis, Tennessee, under the leadership of Apostle William "Bill" Adkins. She travels throughout the country preaching and motivating people in worship services, conferences, workshops and seminars. Her unique "Keep It Real" style captivates her audiences and entices them to receive her testimony and embrace her unique ways of ministering. Rest assured, the reason she is a much-sought-after evangelist is because once she is done delivering profound, prophetic and powerful messages, bowed down heads are lifted, troubled minds are at ease, wounded spirits are healed, broken hearts are mended and captives are set free. She believes that once people are inspired and encouraged, they will begin to walk victoriously in the destiny and divine purpose that God has ordained for their life.

Rhonda and her family currently reside in Covington, Tennessee, which is located approximately thirty-five miles north of Memphis. To schedule Rhonda to speak at your church or to your women's group or organization, contact:

Rhonda Hurst

P.O. Box 159

5910 Mt. Moriah, Suite 113

Memphis, Tennessee 38115

Email: rhondabhurst@bellsouth.net